when he leaves you

MICHAELA ANGEMEER

michaelaangemeer.com

Cover art by Suhaila Baheyeldin

ISBN: 978-1-7752727-0-0

for nana

when you are weeping
that is the time to
keep writing

table of contents

childhood

i was born in
the winter
november
two weeks late
no sun for
two more weeks
just snow

i was born in
the winter
november
it was cold
but my mother
gave her body
kept me warm

i could have
become
anyone

my mother sacrificed the first
seven years of our life together
to be there on sick days with maury
and chicken noodles
to release my brother's
grip from my hair
even when i deserved it
to teach me that
addition and subtraction
would be guiding principles
of my life
not just math
to instill in me a love for words
when they were printed out on pages
to make sure i felt her heartbeat
even when she was
not holding my hand
at choir concerts, dance recitals,
and school assemblies
to show me that a woman could find
true fullness of life in her children
even if they did not realize
what she gave up

stay-at-home mom

favourite memories of dad

trips to home depot
collecting branches
to burn at the cottage
blue and white striped pajamas
glasses with lenses so thick
i filled them with tap water
finding the ocean together
jumping in waves before
i realized how much it
hurts when salt water
stings your eyes

my father is
a good
man

roller coasters at theme parks
unclimbable mountains of red
wrapping paper on christmas eve
a small dog and a big cat
books with words i didn't know yet
pizza and hockey games on the couch
one chocolate chip cookie after dinner
foot rubs and back rubs
kisses on our foreheads
i love you before bedtime

so much of it was magic

you can be anything
you want to be

shoulders
back
don't
stick
out
your stomach

dance class

fat kid,
don't sit on my lap
kid why don't
you wear jeans
kid those sweatpants
make you look fat
kid you're going to eat
another one
kid you finished
the whole bag
kid why are
you crying kid,
it's time to thicken
your fat skin

when my father left my mother
he left a hole in her
she tried to hide it
with her hands
cover it to make
sure nothing spilled
out only let her tears
leak at night when
she thought i could not
feel the ripples the droplets
created in my bedroom
i would try to use my
small hands to help her
cover up the pain but
the hole she had was
more like a canyon
she could not stop me
from falling in and
learning to call emptiness home

i saw vulnerability
drip from my
father's eyes
for the first time
when i was twelve

in that moment
i learned the
sweet sick
balance of
empathy and blame

five
only eat
five things today
count out on fingers
that's six–snap the elastic
on your wrist ten situps ten
jumping jacks repeat repeat
no one's home to hear you heave

how much
s p a c e
should i take up
today

size matters

the problem
with being
brought up
a good
christian girl–
you learn it's normal
to love a man who can't say
he loves you back

i tried to find my father
in different forms
eventually
i realized
no man could
make up for
what he missed

though i put up all these walls myself, each brick placed carefully, i too easily hand over the sledgehammer to knock them down. i always fall willingly, eyes closed. i laugh at knee pads and parachutes. i don't know how to save things for later. i seek out broken people that love breaking and need fixing. i fix them and they break me. i don't know how to save myself. i make these same mistakes over and over again, 'cause no one ever taught me the value of learning my lesson.

i am my father's daughter

nothing was
more healing
than the day
you told me
you knew
you are part
of who i am

i do not laugh, i roar. i do not think before i speak.
i am a terrible liar. it seems like i hurt people
accidentally, but i know what i am doing. i am
stubborn. my vanity gets in the way of my
intelligence. i am fiercely passionate about being
alive. if you earn my loyalty, i will run into a
burning house for you. i will burn down a house
for you. if i love you, you will feel it.

soy la hija de mi madre

talking just to hear the
sound of your own voice
is not the best way to
be heard

please listen

*you made
him leave
again*

it must be so hard
to love the ones
who are
half of
him

where do
i go to learn
that it is not
my responsibility
to bring you
joy

the things we were never taught

i told you so
is still
our way
of saying
i love you

my mother taught
me that self
love starts
with cleaning
your baseboards

love the parts of you that are often forgotten

as the only other person
who can truly understand
what it's like to belong
to our parents
i thank you endlessly
for teaching me
that i don't have
to be burdened
by what they could
not figure out

to my brother on his wedding day

we
don't
talk about how
we feel enough

my father made so
many mistakes but he
is just human how can
i not keep forgiving the
man who is half of my
word weaving brain my
belief that anything is
possible my
uncontrollable
need to be
near water

my mother summoned
strength from the holes
inside of her sometimes
manifested in ways she
would never admit
she regrets but does
that even matter
anymore have you
seen how after all that
this woman can still love

i love you
with the tears
we have shed together
the blood that ran
through your veins
into mine the laughter
that somehow brings
more tears all the
unconditional love
we still have here

to mom and dad

him

two people and
too many
unknowns
to count
but all it
takes is
one laugh

first date

is it really possible that
i like being with
you as much as
i like being
alone

i hope so

i want to wake
up to your
smile and your
thumb on my cheek

baby, i've always felt
a connection
with the sea
but how is it
that you summon an
ocean between my legs
without even touching me

are you easy to please
when i blurted
out no,
you laughed
out loud
now you know
i wasn't kidding

i'm so used to
temporary
paper people
but you're
helping me
get used to
the idea of
permanence

give me
a warm
easy love

his lap feels like
a safe
place until
he stands up

i clean my apartment before
you come over so you
can't draw any
conclusions
from the mess

don't open the closet doors

oh baby, i wish
i could love
you back but
honestly, all
i know how to
do is write about
unrequited love

why am i trying
to run away
when all
you have
asked
for is
us

please don't
let me
leave

what happens
if i just
stay

i wish
i could look
at you without
seeing everything
i'd like to change

all i
want is a
soft, beautiful
love to write shiny,
glittery words about

all i've got is dark and twisty

leave your expectations
outside the door
i do not want to
meet any of them

your love
for me
is only
exposing
everything
i don't like
about myself

baby,
i've got
so many words
too bad you like me
better when i'm brief

as your fingers make
your way from my
sternum to my
stomach
i flinch
you ask
what's wrong
moving your
hand down to my
hipbone is the only
response i can think of

you asked me
if i liked flowers
i knew you wanted me
to say *no*
so i did
you muttered
they don't last long enough
i still don't know
if that's when you
realized i was also
temporary

there
are spiders
in every corner
of my ceiling i can't
live with your ghosts too

i don't want to know
what it felt like
to be between
their legs

you present your past
lovers to me a fleet
preparing to face the
firing squad if only
you knew my
propensity to
lift up women
when faced with
the opposing
perspectives of war

you are obsessed with
picking things up
putting them down
for years you built
blisters that thickened
on your palms like
moss on forgotten rocks

if you weren't so focused
on your self-perceived
imperfections you might
have noticed my mind
throwing your stones
into the river hoping
to find some depth

he will
never love
you more
than he
loves himself

ask me questions
you are afraid
to know the
answers to
but do not
tell me what
you fear for
i will become it

if a woman says *yes*
when you take her hand
smiles *please* when you
kiss her neck nods *more*
when you slip your fingers
beyond her waistband she
has not opted in to every
unexpected fantasy you
plan to drag her into next

consent

you love women based
on boxes you can
fit their limbs
into

you cracked my walls
but you didn't give me
a good enough reason
to take them down

i will put you on
like a new pair of
shoes walk around
so that my footprints
leave scuffs on your
soles take you off
when i've worn
you down and
never put you
on again

i transformed my body
for you only to
realize it didn't
even want you

what do i do with it now

breaking up with
you was just
another item
on my
to do list

MICHAELA ANGEMEER

our teeth sparkled
bright white when
we first met but you
drank too much black
coffee and i too much
red wine so now these
stains on what used
to be pure white are
all that's left of us

how did i get so
good at
subtraction

i'm sorry that
i used you to
see if i was
worth loving

everything is you

you look like another floor
i could slip on

make me laugh
tell me it is your
favourite sound

your smile
could make
me fall
to the ground
from across a freeway

i need a map
to find the line
between friends
and more than

is it how in a
full room you
look at me first to
see if i am laughing

is it in the way
my cheeks hurt
from smiling at you

is it the eye contact
that seeps past
my eyeline feels
like it might make
its way into my soul

can i use a map
to find this
line or does it
not exist

when he walks into your life you'll realize
everything was black and grey before
he is colour when your eyes are closed
he'll fill your lungs with flames
he'll teach your veins how to carry blood

he'll whisper to your heart,
this is what a pulse feels like

our eyes are the same
shade of chocolate
the crook of your neck
calls me by name
your smile lines only
make mine deeper
the way your hands
put me at ease feels
more natural than the
sky's shade of blue
when god made you
i can't help but think
he had me in mind

i could build a city
with the way
you make me feel
brand new
lay down railways
pepper a downtown core with
historic landmarks imported from
that one little street in san francisco
i was too drunk to
remember the name of
make sure every corner
had a feisty old italian man
or a woman who'd look
past your eyes into your soul
string lights across the alleyways
because everyone here has a balcony
fill all the bodegas with
your favourite red wine
clear the skies at night
so we'd have something
to look at
other than each other

i will take down
these walls for you
if you promise
to build a home in me

i am in pieces
the smallest fragments
too small to be broken
again but
you are slow
soft and patient
and my pieces are
starting to feel
like parts of a whole

how did you figure me out

baby, i've peeled off my skin for you
i'm ripping away muscle
give me a moment
to crack open my rib cage
i have no use for
these bones anymore
excuse me while i
cut through veins
sever arteries
i think i've almost got it now
it's pulsing in my palm
here, take my heart
it's better off with you

i do not know how
it feels to fall in
love all i do is
drown in it

you are my yayo's paella
a sweater that's too big
my favourite pair of jelly shoes
my father coming home in time for dinner
the way i laughed before i knew it was too loud
the stuffed toy lamb i used to talk to
that one tree i could actually climb
the corner lot
home

i want to build a house
with your breath
paint the walls
with your tongue
make a string of
lights with your teeth
lay the foundation
with the feeling i get
when you say my name

your words are like bricks

i
am
letting
you in more
than you know

you were the
first man
to laugh
right
into
me

you instill in me a
confidence i have
never been able to
find in myself

you are the
realest thing
i have ever felt

love is not magic
i can explain in
full detail the
sinews of my heart
that love you
there are no tricks here
no sleight of hand
there is just pure
raw feeling a me
and a you a patience
and delicateness that
magic could not hide in
a hat there will be no
sawing in half only us
joining together they
say love is magic but
how i feel about you
is not an illusion

i'm so good
at fixing let me
kiss those tears away

i can turn water into moonlight

i know you've never planted
a tree but i can show you a
thing or two about
putting down roots

if you cannot want me because
of time, space, or circumstance

undo us in your mind
unravel me from your words
unwrap me from around your finger

let me go

when i tried to stop thinking
about you i dreamt
your name was
embroidered
all over my
clothing

what does it
feel like to live
under my skin

i did not ask you to
put out the sun with
your fingertips or
pull down the moon
with your gaze for me
or catch the stars with
your tongue and yet
you did anyway

truthfully, i don't know what else i wanted

i can't possibly believe
that god chose
you and i
to drown
in the same river
with no intention
of helping us
find what
we need to
build a raft

rapids

i've put myself
back together
so many times
i don't mind
if you break
me again

just let me feel something

i am trying to build
a bridge with my heart
but i do not know
if i will use it
to get to you
or get over you

help me decide

we can
just be
us

when you asked the street
lights to burn brighter
for you did you
even think
about how
quickly
they'd
erase
my
stars

selfish

i am not a piece
by piece person
i want all of you
or nothing at all

you never said
you loved me
but i felt it

i might believe
that every place
contains a certain
number of poems
i found one when
i dropped my clothes
on your bedroom floor
and picked them up
the next morning
there are words
waiting for me
in the park
where i wanted
to hold your hand
but didn't
i can count the syllables
created by your pulse
in the coffee shop
across the train tracks
and there is more
than a dictionary could hold
on the floor where i sat
when you told me
you were leaving

drink everything
like it's wine and
he's pouring it

when he leaves you

over

there are different types
of crying sometimes
small drops drip
from your eyes can
be wiped away easily
with a fingertip forgotten

there are loud sobs
of crocodile tears
floods of wet face
dehydration makes
you fall asleep

crying for you cracked
open my spine hunched
over i fell to the floor part
of my soul screamed its
way out of me i could
not fathom a reason
to stand up i could
not figure out where all
the water was coming from

weeping

my summer skin
is gone but you
are still all
over me

the first snowfall
never fails to remind me
of falling into you
it was not soft white powder
barely covering the pavement
my fall was a thud
like the chunks of ice
that will come
when it's colder
this fall was
a million pieces of me
bouncing off your windshield
you had seen snow fall
before but you were not
ready for my hail

nothing makes
me feel as
warm as
you did

when you
first left
i could not
eat for three
days would
you have stayed
if i was smaller

brazilian waxes. plucking eyebrows. digging at ingrown hairs. pulling out splinters. convulsing with stomach cramps. biting the inside of your cheek. stubbing your baby toe on the corner of the coffee table. a paper cut from freshly printed pages. tripping over high heels, bloodying your knee.

nothing hurts more than heartbreak

it's one pm on a sunday
i'm drunk because i
mixed beer with cider
while cooking roasted
potatoes trying to poach
eggs perfectly

i'm drunk because making
breakfast reminds me
of you but still you're
not here and the tipsy
in me has always
been good company

he wants you
to learn how
to be yourself
without him

don't focus on the leaving

when you ran away
i really thought i would
run too but i've got
roots made out of lead
and a heavier heart than
either of us knew

can i
really blame
you for leaving
if i'm the
one who
let go

can i
really blame
you for leaving
if i never held
on in the
first place

i put my feet in the ocean
float on my back
pray
think of you anyway

you come to me in waves

hello,
are you ready to love me yet?

can i use your bones
to start a fire
on nights when
i feel you next to me
but you are not
really there

i just want to breathe in your smoke

i thought we were
puzzle pieces
fit together perfectly
turns out you're just
square and i've got
too many holes carved
out of me for us to ever
see the bigger picture

stop trying to fill
your cracks
with his
good intentions

leave them empty for a while

i pity you for
not being able
to fall in love with
this world and its
beautiful flaws

don't you worry, baby
your love
for him
will fade
like always

i really don't think
you miss me
but do you miss
the way i could
make you laugh

like no one else

i still have that scar
from when you
made me trip
over my words
there's a small
mark on my right
earlobe from when
you whispered
we're the same
i can't seem to get
rid of the sore on
the back of my throat
from when you asked me
to swallow my tongue and i
don't think this burn on my
chest from loving you more than a human
should love a wildfire will ever go away

the river is
overflowing
there is too
much rain
for us to
stand anymore
even if god sent
us a sailboat it
would surely
capsize

i can still
feel your
laugh on
the inside
of my
rib cage

if you sweep someone
off their feet you
are supposed to
catch them

you said our souls
were the same
and you seared
yours to mine
then you left
and you pulled
off my skin
so all i have
is raw, bare bones
but at least i have nothing
to hide behind anymore

thank you for exposing me

i am tired
of mourning
what we could have
been when we were never
meant to amount to anything

every night i whisper
to the dreamcatcher
pinned above my bed
please don't let me
dream of him
its feathers
molt in response

i'm scraping away
my insides making
room for you within
the walls of my heart
my blood is so full of
oxygen now it would
make great soil for you
i would be the perfect place
for you to plant your roots

please come back

i miss the
way you used
to smile for me

ear to ear, all teeth

i will always
find you
near water

when
he makes
you feel like
you still matter
to him you are
lying to yourself

when he makes you
feel like lying
to yourself
let him go

if only you saw the way
my eyes sparkled
for you took in
light that danced
across my pupils
reflected back into yours

if only you felt the
way my heart beat for
you hard and fast the
way it moved heat
across my skin

if only you looked
closely enough to
realize my smile for
you was so wide
it could have
swallowed the skyline

if only you stopped
for a second to
really see me
you could have had
all of me

i cannot be your
red flag i am
my own
siren

i fell in love
with a version
of you that
does not exist

turns out loving me
is not hard but
leaving me
is easy

i hope the women
who come after me
know better than
to fall at your feet
when you call them
the yin to your yang

you remind me of
overpriced coffee
second guessing myself
that red drawstring hoodie
unreliability and
sentences strung
together poorly

so why am i still
writing about you

i try to play you off
as a phase
an infatuation
but you are
not someone
who brushes off
easily you are
an enigma
an entity
a lifelong muse

bit by bit i removed
you from my life
wiped the part of
my memory that
stored your smell
deleted the mental
picture i took of your
smile recorded over
the track that played
your laugh over and
over now all that's
left is an empty space
where my feelings for
you used to live

when he comes back
don't you dare
forget how you
broke when
he left

my love for you could
have overflown a river
or filled the ocean it
could have changed
tides convinced the
earth to revolve around
the moon my love could
have lived longer than
the north star it could have
reversed the earth's poles
but you were not ready for it
when you let me go
my scream shook the
sky i swear all the stars
fell out of it scorched
the atmosphere
the moon could not
be seen even though
it was supposed to be full
the sun gave up on rising
the next morning but still
she whispered to me,

it's not that you don't
love him anymore,
it's that you can't

repairing

i often
accuse people
of leaving me but
i am always the one
telling them
to go

part of
being broken
is wanting to be

putting yourself
back together
is a choice

if you take
two steps
back for
every two
steps forward
you are standing still

just let
yourself be
lonely

i went to
a palm reader
and a therapist

they both
asked me
why i doubt myself

universal truths

i never talk about you
most people don't know
you exist in me
because it hurts
to call you by name

you're inconsistent
worry has a purpose
you whisper don't look
them in the eye look them
in the eye you should smile
more there are too many
people here in this room

no one wants to talk to you
listen to me don't leave yet
you can go wait–go back
now they're mad at you
i'm mad at myself
why are you like this

meet my anxiety

one day you're fine
visiting the grocery store
you don't even think
about looking the
cashier in the eye
you just do

then you can't even
drive to work without
rehearsing your answers
to the most mundane
questions

how are you?

when you feel
the need to
leave wait
fifteen more minutes

does everybody
feel like this
sometimes

you don't have
to dig at your
roots to get
better

therapy lessons

the doubt is so persistent
you might not even notice her
fluttering eyelashes not-so-subtle
whispers she blends in with
do i belong heres and why am i
trying to fold into myself why
aren't i speaking louder why
do all my sentences
end in a question when
i know i am right
i know i am smart
i know i make good decisions
i am more worthy than i have ever been

why does she still get to live here
when everyone else has left

if only i could
trade this body
for a body of
water float
out so far that
my curves become
one with the waves

i've always let
my emotions
create storms
within me
but you turned
my thunder
into a hurricane

if only
i could
exist in
a vacuum

time
heals
every
open wound

what do i do with the ones i closed

how could you build up
this brightness in me
make me shine like i never had
then smash my bulbs
crush filaments
leave me shattered
this gas leak went unnoticed
i left my mask in a box
with all the boys before you
you promised i would not need it
i can't believe i thought we were soulmates
i can't believe this is what you do for fun
i stopped playing games when i was a child
how as an adult have you
made a life out of them
the worst part is it took me
so long to smell the wretch
of what you left over
you are where the doubt came from
you are why i questioned my purpose
if you dare come back beware
i have an army of self worth now
a firing squad of confidence
the shoulders of the giants you stand on
belong to me

gaslighted

i am tired
the rain drops
keep singing
it is time for sleep
but there are
still words
pouring out
of me

don't fall asleep yet

when you are weeping
that is the time to
keep writing

there is room
for your words here
do not silence yourself

baby,
you do not
have to be so
hard on yourself

the cracks in
your shell
let the light in

this is not all beautiful
it is not all water
roots and metaphors
sometimes it is a red ladybug yoga
mat mushrooms stuffed with
breadcrumbs and cheese
a messy bun an eye infection
leftover pad thai with no more shrimp
shaking hands at midnight from the
latte i drank at three
tears when i cannot
get it right no sleep
unless it feels right
but i guess the point
is not finding beauty
when it is easy

with shaking hands i am
untying the thread
you left around
my heart

please don't pull on me anymore

on days like this i wear
my mother's sweatshirt
that i took from her
closet when i was sixteen
it is a day for unwashed hair
in a top knot and a weak
attempt at winged eyeliner
today my lips are chapped
and my latte tastes like
burnt coffee beans today
is not a good day but
today is the first day where
i only thought of you once

don't focus
so much on addition
and subtraction the only
math that matters is
finding your equal

you deserve
love deeper
than the ocean

do not settle for a stream

i was waiting for you
but my self worth
showed up
instead

who knew you'd be so easy to replace

learning how to love myself
is possibly more
burdensome
than it was to
forget how
to love
you

días sin amor

hearts that are
broken can be
rebuilt

diving into love quickly
so fast your nose hits
the ocean floor makes
rising out of love like
drowning over and over
until you remember all
you have to do is float
to the surface to get
back to yourself

don't let anyone
switch your
love light
to off
again

protect it at all costs

i dyed my hair blonde
to bleach away the
memories of my childhood
no one will recognize you
now it is time to replace
the bleach let my roots grow
dark like my mother's and
her mother before her
anoint my head with oil
nourish my hair the way
i should have all along

it will always
hurt but you
will move on

baby, your beauty is beyond
the earth's surface
the galaxies look
to you to learn
how to shine

i found a box today
i was nervous to
look inside but it
pulled me in with the
promise of the unknown
i slid scissors across
the tape and pulled the
flaps apart at first
i could not recognize
the contents then
i felt a shiver of
you are worth the world and
a tingle of *you can be tender*
and when i heard
your love is so great
you deserve to feel it
for yourself
my eyes watered as
i took self love from the box
let it glow in the palm of my hand
and vowed to never box it up again

perspective

every part of losing
a loved one is the
hardest part but
nothing feels
heavier than
knowing it
is coming

i would breathe
all the air in my lungs
into yours if i could
share my heartbeat with you
i wish i could walk down every
street in pontevedra pick the
flowers you picked
cuando eras una niña
braid them together
make you a crown
queens live forever,
don't they

para mi nana, eres la reina de mi alma

how did god wrap
so much love into
such a small woman

four foot eleven

when i was a teenager
i beamed with pride
when i hit five feet
más alta que nana

oh how i wish i knew
then that her height
was the least important
part of her i should
aspire to become

when i find
the right one
voy a escribir
sobre él para ti

nana took a piece of yarn tied
it around yayo's wrist said
we are one
he became whole
she took that same piece
made a wish to god
yayo's hands in hers
god nodded
gave her five more strands
my mother three brothers one sister
she made a patchwork blanket
they all slept in learned what being safe
feels like what it means to build a home
thirty-one years later my mother took her piece
wrapped it around my baby finger whispering
never forget that love can patch any hole

my nana looked
at my yayo like
he was the only
man her eyes
could see he was
her heartbeat her
reason to wake up
in the morning her
last goodnight
her permission
to let go

sesenta y dos años

during your last
day on earth
you broke the
record for
apologizing

all i could
muster in
response was
i love you and
i am so happy to be here

you have given
your love to this
earth even when
you leave it i will
feel for your pulse in

feliz navidad
homemade
empanadillas
tortillas cream puffs
half moon cookies

phone calls just to
say goodnight
thank yous to
inanimate objects
every dog i let lick my face

in every i love you
i feel from now on

it's okay to go now

i imagine god
creating the space
for my nana in
heaven it is
more than
pearly gates and
pure white clouds
he has shaped a new kingdom just
for people who can love like her

ella es la reina

look at
all the love
we have here

cut up an apple and dip it in peanut butter. meditate in a bathtub filled with bubbles. make scrambled eggs with cheese at midnight. smile in the mirror. laugh at yourself when you're alone. buy new underwear. don't wear underwear. learn how to speak a new language. put on makeup and don't go anywhere. sing karaoke while lying in bed. exercise and don't tell anyone about it. do something nice for someone and don't tell anyone about it. call your grandma. visit a body of water. drive on the highway with all your windows down. scream. learn how to love the you no one else sees.

my last words for now to you, dear reader

acknowledgements

i will never take for granted all of you who stayed. thank you, mom and dad, for showing me that humans are flawed, but that's what makes them beautiful and worth loving. thank you for eloquently dealing with the discomfort of me writing about you and supporting me regardless. to my brother, jacob, thank you for comic relief and relentless advocacy of my writing. to my nana, thank you for being the definition of unconditional love for me during the eighty-seven stunning years of your life. to chinye, thank you for being a constant pulse, even when you're hundreds of miles away. to charlotte, thank you for always caring and for being my second set of eyes. to suhaila, thank you for creating a cover more beautiful than i could have ever imagined. to my friends, thank you for supporting me even when i told you i was going to start posting poetry on instagram. i appreciate your encouragement more than you know. to my readers, thank you for connecting with me and never being afraid to share your stories. you mean so much to me. and to everyone who left. thank you for inspiring me to write this book.